Firemark

poems by

Jessica M. Brophy

Finishing Line Press
Georgetown, Kentucky

Firemark

Learn about your inner self from those who know such things, but don't repeat verbatim what they say.

—*"The Phrasing Must Change," Jelaluddin Rumi*

The energetic executive smile, the preacher's pious frown, the doctor's paternal smirk, the sweet-17 pout of the fading beauty— these are the top-layer masks that vanish at the first touch of relaxation, pain, or a double martini.

—*The Zen of Seeing, Frederick Franck*

Copyright © 2018 by Jessica M. Brophy
ISBN 978-1-63534-514-8 First Edition
All rights reserved under International and Pan-American Copyright Conventions.
No part of this book may be reproduced in any manner whatsoever without written permission from the publisher, except in the case of brief quotations embodied in critical articles and reviews.

ACKNOWLEDGMENTS

"Mrs. Hennessey" is published in a chapbook, *The Paper Girl*, with Finishing Line Press (2016).
"Ode to Gerard Manley Hopkins" is published in the *Women's Voices Anthology* with These Fragile Lilacs Press (2017).

Publisher: Leah Maines
Editor: Christen Kincaid
Cover Art: Daniel Brophy
Author Photo: Megan Davies
Cover Design: Jessica M. Brophy

Printed in the USA on acid-free paper.
Order online: www.finishinglinepress.com
also available on amazon.com

Author inquiries and mail orders:
Finishing Line Press
P. O. Box 1626
Georgetown, Kentucky 40324
U. S. A.

Table of Contents

Beltane 1
Mrs. Hennessey 2
Self 3
Portraits 4
A Gang 5
Mother's Hands 6
Sweating Langston Hughes 7
Smacked 8
Candela Laser 9
Seussical 10
Mental Mash 11
Nerve 12
Warning 13
Road Wear 14
Determined to Begin Again 15
Name Calling 16
The Truth I Hide 17
Ode to Birthmark 18
Creation Story 20
Meeting with Mom after a Two-Month Hiatus 21
Anthem 23
The Gaze of Strangers 24
Pock Mark 25
Mapping 26
Little Fire 27
Luck of an Ordinary Day 28
Dear Holy Base of Desire 29
Under the Bodhi Tree 30
Ode to Gerard Manley Hopkins 31
Ars Poetica #1 32
Heaven, Unconditionally 33
Notes 34

BELTANE

Every year, over cake, candles, and a crowd (so she has an audience again), mother tells a story about the time she was in labor with me and Matt on May first.

She announces to the people: *I have to tell you Matt and Jessie's birth story.* Her eyes are mirrors of jouissance, hypsos, memoria calidad, as if she has already traveled back to the brick tenement on Harrison Street and is in labor two weeks early. *I got up around 6 a.m. and felt the urge to push. I got in the shower and then laid back down in the bed. I told Alli, Jessie's 6-year-old sister, to go get the neighbor Gladys. I realized I was in labor and the babies were coming fast! Gladys didn't believe Alli, so I told her to go get Louise who lived down the block. Louise helped me deliver Matt. As soon as he came out, he pee'd straight up in the air, and I said "Look! It's a boy!"* She erects her index finger into the air to show how straight his pee was.

The cop arrives. He thought I was done, but I told him I was having twins. *Jessie came about fifteen minutes later. She slid out with a veil over her head and came butt first. I didn't even have to push. Jessie has a birthmark on her face.* Mother touches above right eye, the bridge of her nose and above the lip to show the crowd where it is. *We always joke and say Matt was wrestling with her in the womb.*

When mother is met by shoppers in the grocery store weeks after delivering the twins, she can confirm that she was the woman on the front page of *The Daily Journal* holding her twins like trophies she won for attending La Leche League. *I felt like a celebrity around town.*

I process mother's recollection that *We always joke.* I understand that family didn't want to bring attention to my birthmark. They were probably thinking: she's healthy, she's normal, she's a special companion to her brother. Why make a big deal about it? *At least you don't have a protuding lesion on the back of your head. Be grateful for that,* mother reminds her.

MRS. HENNESSEY

Mom has rubber-banded my stack
already waiting on the front porch,
with baby Ben in his play pen.
A paper girl in training.

The foyer where I wait to be buzzed in
doesn't mix well with the smell of newspaper ink on my fingertips.
The ink's warm pungency and band's vinegar bite
collide with cheap carpet and microwaved food being prepared inside.
You let me in after you ask, "Who is it?" and I sing, "Pay-purr Gurrrl."

Seniors at the Clifford Case Apartments sit relaxed in the lobby,
their bums enjoying the boxed chairs you'd find
next to a college dormitory's vending machine.

I knock on your door. You answer it, using the help of your walker.
Like every day before, I wait to be rewarded with two
      Twizzler cherry sticks.
You ask me today, *What happened to your face? It looks like
      you got into a fight.
Did someone punch you?*

I am 10 or 11.
I don't have the language
or awareness to tell you
that my face was born with these marks—
a port-wine birthmark, or a stain if you like.
Instead, my body reacts to your nosy questions.
My throat swells up and my eyes fill with warm tears.

Do I look injured?
Strangers pity me?
I leave not knowing how
to narrate what others see.

SELF

I am looking back at me
in eighth grade.
I am wearing boat-neck blouse,
silver geometric hoops.
Some would call the eyebrows unkept.

I am looking straight at her.
She is ready for a head shot.
The whites of my eyes are bright.
She has a closed-mouth smile.
I am wearing cherry lipstick,
new applied over old.
Her eyes say snap the photo.
Capture the light bouncing
underneath my eyes.

I like how her long hair
falls behind her back.
She sees what
I've forgotten—
her birthmark doesn't
seem out of place.
It isn't competing,
even with the inflamed
whitehead under her nostril.

I see a proud chin,
her smile not suspicious
my joy easy.
She is experimenting
with face.
Freckles crawl up
the many bridges of the nose.
Neck is exposed.
She is looking at life,
staring back at her.

PORTRAITS

I am looking at her in tenth grade.
She has strained sophistication.
The camera is further away so
I can't see the color of her eyes.
She has short "Rachel" hairdo,
with bad do-it-yourself blonde
highlight gone orange.
Her neck is turned at a micro-angle,
chin tucked,
lips Rum Raisin.

She is smiling with a closed-mouth again
hiding a set of braces.
Her eyes look meek, her shoulders weak.

Her skin has no imperfections.
She has covered up
her birthmark with Revlon Colorstay: ivory 01.
She looks a little frightened, her head retreating
like a turtle, her eyes not relaxed.
At one time I would have mistaken
her smile for a smirk.

I see that she is fitting in.
She is protecting herself.
She is looking at the photographer
slightly suspicious
of how he will portray her,
and how a flinch in her movements
could make for awkward.

A medium close up shot
shows arms close to body.
She is probably
cupping hands
on her lap.

A GANG

When I was fifteen years old, I was finally part of a gang of girls. We were a conglomerate of second or third generation immigrant whiteness—although we were not trying to preserve anything but American snobbery. We were a crew—girls with last names *Bobenchik* and *Juzwick* need not apply. Chrissy, Cindy, Kelly, and Tara were the girls who wrote in my yearbook. These were the girls who had boyfriends who were athletes. These were the girls who ate lunch with me. The girls who carried brushes in their backpacks. The girls the male teachers stared at. I wanted to be one of them. I wanted to subsume myself into their whiteness, become a drop in this homogenized carton of milk. I wanted to silence any name too harsh sounding. I wanted to ignore everyone and everything that was different.

MOTHER'S HANDS

I remember how reliable my mother's hands were. Creamy colored. Light blue veins pushing up softly below the knuckle ridge. Gelatin nails. Frontier fingers. She patted many chests with those hands, held our collar bones in a full embrace with those hands, pushed the sturdy carriage around with those hands. It is through the touch of her hands that I learn how to soothe lovers with my hands, wipe away tears with my fingertips, hold a pencil tenderly with my hands, take delight in comparing my light blue veins to an earthworm.

SWEATING LANGSTON HUGHES

What happens to a body
that stops sweat?

Does the body absorb toxins?
Will other holes seep sweat instead?
Will it appear in poop?
Does the heart weaken?
Will the throat still swallow saliva?

Does the body of the person say
I will be a writer
so I don't have to move?
Does she miss out
on the life of a
sous chef,
fire-woman,
zookeeper,
borderless doctor,
back-breaking keeper of the vineyard,
captain of her tennis team,
mother in labor?

Will the body build a cooling wall
and insist I will not be moved?
I will not accelerate my heart.
I will not live in a tropical climate.
I will not get excited.
I will control the air around me.
I will choose sedentary
so the body is always cooling.

SMACKED

God never took the time to clean up his mess on my face. This tomato splat isn't elegantly crimson or cheerfully strawberry or sexy cherry or demure mauve or electric fuchsia. He's been throwing tomatoes at me while I perform on the stage of life. A silly Shakespearean fool. The tomato gets attention, but not because it's attractive. It's meant to launch scrutiny. We're the recipients of all that shock, puzzlement, deliberation—people's reaction to seeing our birthmarks. They're looking at you; you're looking at them. You are the shock. Feeling bright red and hot and scared like your face is going to combust into flames then melt into shame.

CANDELA LASER

On the operating table, no place to hide. Only a promise. I put on a pair of goggles and hear the crackle of pebbles receding to the shoreline. Doctor holds laser like a wand and pulses on and off, 1000 times this session. Doctor targets purple stain with laserlabor. Bang bang bang bang. Sky is black with faint bursts of lightening. The wand's energy passes safely through the skin absorbing only pigment in the red blood cells. This is good. Television on with no sound, just a fuzzy screen buzzing with white and black dots. Yellow light heats up blood, which makes it congeal, then waste away, reabsorbed back into the blood stream. This is good. Lighter color underneath the skin. Good. Squeal when the doctor zaps sensitive spots on the face, like above the lip. Toes are curling and everything feels hot hot hot hot.

SEUSSICAL

We dish ourselves generous servings of corn fritters, wellingtongs, and fried green tomaters from the buffet. Where I sit, the hydrangeas have mopheads, the bridesmaids are in periwinkle, and the fiddling quartet makes me feel like I am under the stars. Purple haze and pink clouds are all around, and chopped off tree branches with chia heads pop out of their stumps. I am one of those wearing periwinkle and feel ready to dance.

Uncle Jimmie sits down next to me, asking a question that is naively imagined, insensitive, and strangely circumventive before landing on the amygdala's bullseye. *Didn't you used to have a birthmark?* It's the type of question that catches me off guard, seems harmless to an outsider. I hope nobody heard him. I never think about my birthmark and am not used to being asked personal questions about it. The question itself asserts his control over what we talk about, and I, a twenty four year-old kid, barely a woman, manage to swallow my fear and get out:. "I still do," gulping the words back down as soon as I release them. *Well. You can't tell. You do a good job of covering it up.*

The old cover up adage. Like I had a wocket in my pocket or oobleck up my sleeve. Yes. That was it all along. I enjoy covering up. I enjoy the ritual of loathing myself so much I do it every morning at the mirror.

MENTAL MASH

Want I don't different be. Be I want different don't. Face without makeup don't like my. Don't face makeup without my like I. Smiles men won't without makeup. Bed I rolled out feel just makeup without. I'll feel like bed head toothpaste sour mouth. Bite won't it. It's not a bleeding heart. Won't it bite. It's not a Crimson Hand. Be want I don't different. Be I am different. Want I be loved. But I don't love myself. I loved to be want. But I don't love myself. Be loved I want to. I don't want to be different. Loved want I to be. I want to love me.

NERVE

I have a lack of nerve. Tiny blood vessels supposed to constrict or widen so blood rises to the skin's surface don't have nerve either. To be more precise, they lack nerve fibers, which normally keep the vessels narrow. In later stages of development while I swam in utero, some capillaries spilled over, kept expanding, pooling, pooling blood under the skin, and forming my birthmark. Over time, the birthmark grew and became brighter, and more purple and even rougher in some spots. It feels alive and breathing, organic and fixed.

I'm nervous about telling Tj I have a birthmark. We are in the front seat of the car. I get up the nerve and say, *I have to tell you something. It's really hard for me to say this. I don't tell a lot of people . . . I have a birthmark.* "Really? Where?" It is underneath my makeup, so he can't see it. I point quickly to the side of my nose, below my eyebrow, and above my lip, then look at him hoping he will say something that doesn't make me feel ugly. He says, "It's no big deal. Come inside."

Tj doesn't have any furniture in the living room. Just grey carpet. We do snow angels in the middle of the floor. When we're inside a little longer, and I wash off the makeup, he sees it for the first time, and tells me that the mark gives me character. He looks at me, not my birthmark, when he says it. He's not investigating it or stuttering to ask questions that hide what bothers him. He doesn't say he doesn't notice it either. He says he sees it and it adds to my beauty, to me.

"I'm used to seeing things like that in my country. Lots of poor Nigerian boys, including myself, have big belly buttons at birth." He pulls up his shirt and shows me. It looks like a mini-brown water balloon. "We'd all run around without any shirts on playing soccer and we'd notice one another's belly buttons. My cousin, Niyi, was born with a big head too. I don't know if it's a birth defect, but he's had a big head ever since he was born."

He moves on. "Do you want dinner? I can make chicken stew."

WARNING

In abandoned car on side of road,

    red towel sticking out window,

    bloody.

Don't turn my face when someone approaches to help:

    S.O.S.

    aborted.

ROAD WEAR

Have you come to hideaway
or for more hullabaloo?
Are you brokedown
or rippon heart
to let loneliness
come along too?

No wakey wakey.
Not too conched.
You are crooked,
circa 1982.
The sea marking
is, as they say,
a last resort.

It's 5 o'clock somewhere,
if you want to go to Lisa's Clambake,
if you want to walk down Tom's Lane
Want to crash at Park's Pad?

Then there's the bay view.
Wakey wakey.

DETERMINED TO BEGIN AGAIN

I woke up last night.
Things in my head
needed to reach
the blank page,
the new day.

The pain of not changing
is greater
than the pain
of becoming.

I can no longer
lie to myself,
betray myself,
act like I don't
see the birthmark.

When I awake,
Tj asks me
if I want to go for a jog.
The old me would have
made excuses.

Today, it is as if
I want others to see me.
I want to show off.

I rehearse how to respond
to inquiring passerbys:
It's a birthmark.
I was born with it.
Don't see this every day, do ya?
It's interesting right?
    a stroke of ingenuity?
    a mini painting?
    crushed roses?
Your head is also sweet
with raspberry filling, no?

NAME CALLING

Seven employees of a local university are sitting at a bar. A woman approaches and asks them what they would call the mark on her face. The scientist, specializing in taxonomy, says, "I'd call it a *nevus flammeus*." The in-house geneticist utters his idea: "Definitely a mutation in the GNAQ gene." The psychologist says, "No. Of course not. Can't you see it's a vascular malformation?" The chaplain meditates: "I can't quite tell. It looks like a vascular anomaly." An eager lab assistant says nervously, "It looks to me like a localized blood vessel problem." The professor of Latin chimes in: "No. It's definitely just a *naevi*, the Latin term used to describe benign lesions on the skin." The seventh member of the group finally weighs in. "You're all being too technical," she says. "Just call it a port-wine stain. It looks just like the burgundy wine my husband spills all over our white carpet!"

THE TRUTH I HIDE

I prefer silence. I prefer spaces of dead crackling air between talking points. I prefer it if she'd just let me look at her and smile. I prefer it if we just listened to the sounds outside together—the basketball bouncing, the kids sucking a yogurt pop, Patches flapping through the cat window. I prefer communicating without words, like we used to, when I was sucking one breast, and Matt was sucking the other one. Incessant words have a way of confusing me, making me unsure of why I've come to visit again, reaffirming that my mother is incapable of reading this daughter's body language.

ODE TO BIRTHMARK

I had finished reading
a chapter from Gatsby
and sipping
hot green strawberry
tea dripping
down my lip when,
in my dream, I
felt I could appreciate
the dapple in you,
the front-lit
snail sitting
on its hip looking
at me smiling,
the red blotch
above my lip butting
the left side of philtrum.

The stroke below my
eyebrow was painted
in a hurry—
an angel's wing,
Picasso's arch,
pink with attitude.

The spot at
the bridge of my nose
looks like
the half of a baby seal,
its flipper swimming
down the nose gliding
from aquatic glory
to marbled rocks.

All through the dream,
the fan was blowing,
the gold breastplate
of a necklace
against the wall
clink-clink-clink-clink-ering sounds—
the sound of a fork
on a champagne flute toasting.

CREATION STORY

I see pink.
Bazooka skin pink.
Baby's soft tongue pink.
Salmon buttered pink.
I don't know if this means
I'm slowly not shocking myself anymore or
I'm seeing myself through the eyes of a girl.

I'm beginning to finally celebrate myself:
like I do with my favorite pink square in the Starbursts bag or
the nub of an eraser unworn or the lotus flower

                                                       floating
                                                            under my
                                                              direction.

MEETING WITH MOM AFTER A TWO-MONTH HIATUS

When I told you I wasn't going to hide,
I wasn't going to be that person
you would confide in,
a daughter who acquiesces,
absorbs your problems,
I could tell you were processing.
But it wasn't your problem, and guilt,
your very own personal punishment,
is a way to ricochet responsibility.

When I said you were accomplice
to my hiding
      silence shame embarrassment,
instead of saying *I'm sorry*
or *I don't remember,*
I remember you deflecting.
I remember you asking:
Are you sure the hiding
      silence shame embarrassment
isn't a symbol for something else?

You meant to sidetrack me.
You wanted me to be that poised
      stoic guarded numb
daughter so you wouldn't have to embrace
the woman I am becoming: confident,
      alive, sharp, unstoppable.

You didn't give me a language to defend myself.
But now I am language.

I am telling you that
shame is not a symbol for something else
other than hatred for myself
and maybe something deeper
but not more shameful—
hating you—
for not noticing
I use words to survive.

ANTHEM

Come muscles. Come ventricles. Come thumping heart. Push out the toxins, the clots, the stoppages. Take the pain. Make it contract. Come muscles. Come ventricles. Come thumping heart. Bring back a life that is bleeding.

THE GAZE OF STRANGERS

I'm not hiding anymore.
Come see. Ask questions,
politely.

Wearing less makeup
means I don't feel like I'm
modeling a mask that requires
moment by moment
maintenance.
Fibers and specks don't get
caught in the crème.
I don't have
to layer the cake powder,
sealing off my pores.

What was supposed to hide
only exposed inside
what I hid from you,
heightened inside me
what I couldn't see,
flashed like a slide show
in the mind's projector
        bathroom mirror
        full length mirror
        compact mirror
everywhere I go
looking for a mirror
        jean section
        sunglass carousel
        rear view
        reflection in the train window.

Looking in mirrors showed me
what you see,
which means
I blinded myself
trying to manage
the gaze of strangers.

POCK MARK

I am the pock mark on
The rubella notebook.
I am the skinny Number
Two pencil.
I am a musky woman
Wishing of Egyptian goddesses.
I am the flaming capillaries
Underneath her own skin. I am the desert
Seeking the sublime. I am silver branches
Hit by sun. I am broken bark
Dissolving into heat.

MAPPING

We've come upon hidden fields
of sunflowers exhilarating,
stopping in Franktown for
an old bottle of Coke
at the oyster docks.

We happen upon manicured
gardens and accidentally bump into
a small village of beach shacks.

Full of fishermen,
boys riding bikes through billowing sheets.

Our escape together.
I finally have Mom's attention.

LITTLE FIRE

On August 28th, 2005, Mary assumed her position to become a mother: she asked me to make phone calls to relatives. She positioned herself on all fours and rocked back and forth during contractions. She chatted with her nurse about Mexican food. My mother, already an expert 8 times over, stood in the background and laughed with the male mid-wife, Martin, a former Mojave Desert Marine. My father shuffled outside Mary's room in his man-made loafers. At 10 p.m., Mary pushed for forty minutes before "little fire" emerged alongside the burst capillaries around her eyes. The umbilical cord—part rotini al dente, part coil wire, part berry ice cream swirl—dangled in front of me. I followed its origin from "little fire's" brown navel to the inside of Mary. I gawked at the transposed jump rope and reveled in the slimy miracle of Aidan's cord.

LUCK OF AN ORDINARY DAY

I helped Mary push the lawnmower up her steep, weedy hill of a front lawn today. I let Maya and Molly rummage through my pocketbook for at least a half an hour. I talked to a guy at a junk yard in Madison Heights so he could order a new regulator for my driver side window. I put up a clothesline with a pulley system, then hung up my pants and Tj's underwear. Our upstairs neighbor told me she was pregnant, but she has a crooked torso, has been spotting a lot, and can't walk up and down the stairs. The fitness instructor at the Y asked me what my name was again.

My former writing student who works at the grocery store draws a blank when it comes time to say hello. He wears a name tag that says "Zac," so I don't blush like he does. "We all should wear name tags," I suggest. "That's a good idea," he chuckles goofily. "I'll write about that."

He rubs the bridge of his nose with his pointer finger at the same time that he asks, "What happened?". "I have a birthmark. I got tired of wearing makeup. It's a good place to be." "I can respect that," he says, putting his head down, grinning and laughing nervously again.

Savannah returns from her shift break. Zac returns to his normal register.

No heart murmurs. No instant sweating. No looking away. No more mind games. Luck of an ordinary day.

DEAR HOLY BASE OF DESIRE,

Let me know when I'm not listening to you. Make my stomach groan. Pinch my neck. Tighten my quadriceps on the way out the door. Release a pulsing pain in my eye.

When my wrists hurt, pray for me. Ask Brigit if I can rest. If she says yes, send me a peace that blesses the resting hands, fingers, knuckles, palms of poets.

When my eyes close, let me see the ocean. Let me smell a mixture of Mom's musky Odyssey and mussels cooked in garlic, jalapeños, and white wine.

Direct the path of these feet. When you let me hug the chest of another, let it be electricity.

Your supplicant, Jessica

UNDER THE BODHI TREE

It is hot morning
underneath the only tree
on Smith Beach.
It sits back on the base
of the dune hills
strewn with pine needles.

I feel alive here.
Shaded without leaves.
Safe with no urgency.
The bay water moves forward
and sips from the rim's lip.
Fire ants make a life
of their own around me.

I do not feel alone here.
It is stark, empty, early.
I prostrate towards the sun
take space around me
feel the yoga mat sticky.

ODE TO GERARD MANLEY HOPKINS
after "Pied Beauty" by Gerard Manley Hopkins

Glory be to goddess for
scabs, moles, pores, pocks,
strawberry marks, wine washes,
bark that sheds,
overgrown trails,
jagged toenails.

Let us all praise her for
coffee stained car seats,
pollen art on dashboards,
paint chipped car doors,
moles on eyelids,
bulbous belly buttons,
eye patched children,
radiation streaks,
across the breast.

Goddess made those
women with big feet
and men with small hands
and for hairs to grow on chins and
crooked mouths to smile.

Praise her
for missing eyelashes,
potholed sidewalks,
shattered stained glass,
fixed and finished with masking tape.
She is the god of all things strange,
rare, blotched, bumpy,
bleeding, changing,
with cherry on top.

ARS POETICA #1

We three women,
minus one warrior who
is helping her mate
carve and paint,
have gathered
to praise alleluia
for one another.

We have gathered—
yet sit alone
at home
in our office abodes.
We talk loudly into the stratosphere
of Google beaming.

We have gathered
to observe thinking with
the tension of twirling
pens through fingers.
Drum majors.

We have come to this screen
to learn the art
of arranging lilacs
letting them settle
upon our friend's delight
and contemplation.

Our hearts are beating,
the kitchen table saving
seats for the next time
we can whisper
and still be heard.

We are here
not to hunt butterflies
but to know feelings flitter
when our words pass through
the bodies of one another.

HEAVEN, UNCONDITIONALLY

I am splashing. Sun hits my face. I hear birds hatching. We make jokes about the marks on our bodies. *Your birthmark's so bumpy, even a car on the AutoBahn would slow down. Your birthmark's so frazzled, it could be Frankenstein's cousin.* We are children who make art out of our marks. A Venus de Milo with a birthmark shaped like a ladybug on her left cheek. A Mona Lisa with strawberries kissing her right eyebrow and gogi berries rolling down the bridge of her nose. Van Gogh's starry night with a red and purple sunset. Picasso's Ladies of France with arms painted merlot, burgundy, pinot noir. Beauty is born again and again in interlocking swirls on the beach. We dance to polyrhythmic beats and wear necklaces formed by sweat beads.

Notes

On the title: "A port-wine stain (*nevus flammeus*), also commonly called a firemark, is almost always a birthmark . . . It is caused by a vascular anomaly (a capillary malformation in the skin). Port-wine stains are named for their coloration, which is similar in color to Port-wine, a fortified red wine from Portugal" (Wikipedia entry).

"Beltane": Also known as May Day or May 1st, it is celebrated throughout Gaelic regions as the halfway point between the spring equinox and summer solstice. Bonfires are lit as a ritual because they are said to protect the livestock and future crop growth. Miriam Dyak says, "Beltane is a traditional time to renew, reawaken our fire—inner fire, hearth fire, community fire, sexual and fertility fire of people, animals, plants, and the land."

"Smacked": The tomato color of Paolo Freire's *Pedagogy of the Oppressed* (1968) inspired me to write this poem. At the time, I could not be that woman to revolutionize how we learn, living a life of inquiry that rejects rote information. I was not ready to reject the formula that Freire says we must if we are to be full participants in the world.

"Candela Laser": Most dermatology web sites liken the feel of a candela laser to a rubber band snapping against the skin. In the mid 1990s when I went to the plastic surgeon's office for a consultation, each treatment would have cost $750. Since I didn't have treatments as a baby, when the birthmark was smaller, less purple, and less raised, I would now need at least eight to ten treatments to significantly reduce the birthmark's brightness. My parents knew the insurance company, considering it a cosmetic procedure, wouldn't cover the costs. I also later learned that treatments would also need to be repeated over the years, since the blood would once again pool, and my birthmark would reappear. This poem is what I imagined the procedure would feel like.

"Mental Mash": Georgiana is a character in Nathaniel Hawthorne's short story, "The Birthmark," (1843, 1846). The birthmark is called a "Crimson Hand" that "blazed forth . . . to scare away all their [marriage's] happiness." Her husband is an alchemist and scientist who is dogged in his attempts to find universal solvents, such as the Elixir of Life. He is also frightened by the birthmark on Georgiana's face. After working night and day in his lab to find a cure to remove the birthmark, the husband administers an elixir to Georgiana, but as the birthmark blanches, she also becomes very pale and dies.

"Road Wear": On my morning walks at Smith Beach in the summer of 2013, I noticed that many of the houses had "name-plate" signs announcing the homeowner's philosophies. I compiled a list of the words on the signs and wrote this poem.

"Anthem": This poem was inspired by what is considered the Unitarian Universalist's anthem, "Spirit of Life." The song inspired me to write my own anthem for living.

Jessica M. Brophy is a poet who writes about the body, family quirks, nature's luster, childhood, and the otherworld. *Firemark* is the sequel to her poetry debut, *The Paper Girl* (Finishing Line Press, 2016). What happens to this girl with a paper route who grew up in a Christian fundamentalist home? Does she find a language to narrate her life? Does she learn to love her body? *Firemark* is the story of how Brophy learns to love the burst of purple and red on her face, finally finding her own seal-skin.

Brophy was the runner-up in Minerva Rising's 2016 Owl of Minerva Award for her poem, "Invocation to Margarets." The poem is part of Brophy's current poetry project which traces the biological Margarets in her family (who can be traced back to County Tyrone in Ireland) and the spiritual Margarets (the Irish female goddesses from ancient mythology). While Brophy is only beginning to understand the ancestors in her present life, and longs for female wisdom to guide her heart, she is not surprised that she comes from a land where poets are revered and women goddesses are poets themselves. After winning the award, Brophy became a memoir reader at Minerva Rising Press.

Subscribe to Brophy's blog at www.beautyfullwriting.com to read more about her writing life and a list of writing consultation services provided to young professional women. Brophy lives in Charlottesville, VA with her husband, Tj.